Wisdom *for* Marriage Stability

"Wherefore they are no more twain, but one flesh.
What therefore God hath joined together,
let not man put asunder."

Mathew 19:6

By
Franklin N. Abazie

Wisdom for marriage stability
COPYRIGHT 2015 by Franklin N Abazie
ISBN: 978:0-9966-263-54

All right reserved. This book or any portion thereof may not be reproduced or used in any manner whatsoever without the express written permission of the publisher, except for the use of brief quotations in a book review. All Bible quotes are from King James Version and others as noted.

Published by:
F N ABAZIE PUBLISHING HOUSE---a.k.a,
Empowerment Bookstore:

That I may publish with the voice of thanksgiving and tell of all thy wondrous works.
Psalms26:7

To order additional copies, wholesales or booking:
Call the Church office (973-372-7518)
or Empowerment Bookstore Hotline 973-393-8518

Worship address:
343 Sanford Avenue Newark New Jersey 07106
Administrative Head Office address:
33 Schley Street Newark New Jersey 07112
Email:pastorfranknto@yahoo.com
Website www.fnabaziehealingministries.org
Publishing House: www.fnabaziepublishinghouse.org

This book is a production of F N Abazie Publishing House. A publication Arms of Miracle of God Ministries 2019
First Edition

CONTENTS

The Mandate of The Commission.....................iv

Favor Confession vi

Introduction....................................viii

CHAPTER 1
Asking God in Prayers for our God Ordained Spouse............................... 18

CHAPTER 2
Understanding God's Chosen Spouse for You..28

CHAPTER 3
Prayer of Salvation............................ 60

CHAPTER 4
About The Author 68

Books By Rev Franklin N Abazie..................... 70

THE MANDATE OF THE COMMISSION

"THE MOMENT IS DUE TO IMPACT YOUR WORLD THROUGH THE REVIVAL OF THE HEALING & MIRACLE MINISTRY OF JESUS CHRIST OF NAZARETH."

"I AM SENDING YOU TO RESTORE HEALTH UNTO THEE AND I WILL HEAL THEE OF THY WOUNDS, SAID THE LORD OF HOST."

ARMS OF THE COMMISSION

1) F N Abazie Ministries-Miracle of God Ministries (Miracle Chapel Intl)
2) F N Abazie TV Ministries: Global Television Ministry Outreach.
3) F N Abazie Radio Ministries: Radio Broadcasting Outreach.
4) F N Abazie Publishing House: Book Publication.
5) F N Abazie Bible School: also called Word of Healing Bible School (W.O.H.B.S)
6) F N Abazie Evangelistic Ass: Miracle of God Ministries: Global Crusade
7) Empowerment Bookstore: Book distribution.
8) F N Abazie Helping Hands: Meeting the help of the needy world wide
9) F N Abazie Disaster Recovery Mission: Global Disaster Recovery.
10) F N Abazie Prison Ministry: Prison Ministry for all convicts "Second chance"

Some of our ministry arms are waiting the appointed time to commence.

FAVOR CONFESSION

Father thank you for making me righteous and accepted through the blood of Jesus Christ. Because of that, I am blessed and highly favored by God. I am the subject of your affection. Your favor surrounds me as a shield, and the first thing that people see around me is your favored shield.

Thank you that I have favor with you and man today. All day long people go out of their way to bless me and help me. I have favor with everyone that I deal with today. Doors that were once closed are now opened for me. I receive preferential treatment, and I have special privileges, I am Gods favored child.

No good thing will he withhold from me. Because of Gods favor my enemies cannot triumph over my life. I have supernatural increase and promotion. I declare restoration to everything that the devil has

Favor Confession

stolen from my life. I have honor in the midst of my adversaries and an increase in assets, especially in real estate and expansion of territories.

Because I am highly favored by God, I experience great victories, supernatural turnarounds, and miraculous breakthrough in the midst of great impossibilities. I receive recognition, prominence, and honor. Petitions are granted to me even by ungodly authorities. Policies, rules, regulations, and laws are changed and reverse on my behalf.

I win battles that I don't even have to fight, because God fights them for me. This is the day, the set time and the designated moment for me to experience the free favor of God, that profusely and lavishly abound on my behalf in Jesus name. **Amen.**

INTRODUCTION

> "Two are better than one; because they have a good reward for their labour."
>
> **Eccl4:9**

In my life time, I may never get the chance to meet you in person one to one, but I am glad to meet you here through the pages of this great book. I love the strength of books in print.

"Marriage" have been *misinterpreted* and *misrepresented* by even the very elect. This small book" *WISDOM FOR MARRIAGE STABILITY."* is a book designed to help singles about to *be married, the married and those going through crisis in marriage.* This book is designed to encourage you make the relevant wise decision to stabilize your marriage. We were told……

Introduction

"Two are better than one; because they have a good reward for their labour. For if they fall, the one will lift up his fellow: but woe to him that is alone when he falleth; for he hath not another to help him up.

Again, if two lie together, then they have heat: but how can one be warm alone?

And if one prevail against him, two shall withstand him; and a threefold cord is not quickly broken." **Eccl4:9-12**

In my own opinion, any marriage ordained by God must last for generation to come. It is written "Wherefore they are no more twain, but one flesh. *"What therefore God hath joined together, let not man put asunder."* **Mathew19:6.**

Therefore come with me let us unfold what the *Holy Spirit* is saying concerning a lasting and stable marriage.

Happy Reading

HIS DESTINY WAS THE CROSS....

HIS PURPOSE WAS LOVE....

HIS REASON WAS YOU....

"And said, For this cause shall a man leave father and mother, and shall cleave to his wife: and they twain shall be one flesh?"

Mathew19:5

"Wherefore they are no more twain, but one flesh. What therefore God hath joined together, let not man put asunder."

Mathew 19:6

"The man who hates and divorces his wife," says the Lord, the God of Israel, "does violence to the one he should protect," says the Lord Almighty.

So be on your guard, and do not be unfaithful."

Mal2:16

"Two are better than one; because they have a good reward for their labor."

Eccl4:9

"For if they fall, the one will lift up his fellow: but woe to him that is alone when he falleth; for he hath not another to help him up."

Eccl4:10

"Again, if two lie together, then they have heat: but how can one be warm alone?"

Eccl4:11

"And if one prevail against him, two shall withstand him; and a threefold cord is not quickly broken."

Eccl4:12

CHAPTER 1

ASKING GOD IN PRAYERS FOR OUR GOD ORDAINED SPOUSE

> "But seek ye first the kingdom of God, and his righteousness; and all these things shall be added unto you."
>
> **Mathew 6:33**

It is our *God ordained right* for every man/woman to seek the face of *God in prayer for our potential spouse in life.* "And the Lord God said, It is not good that the man should be alone; I will make him an help meet for him. Genesis2:18

For generation, marriage has always been God ordained institution that has attracted all kinds of argument and

Chapter 1: Asking God in Prayers for our God Ordained Spouse

criticisms. *"Marriage is honourable in all"*. Hebrew 13:4

Among *all these things that shall be added unto you* from the opening scripture is our *potential spouse. As long as there is a man or woman to pray, there is always a God to answer*. As a man or woman ready for marriage, our first assignment in pursuit of our spouse, is to ask God in prayer. *"Diligent prayer unto God comes back with genuine answer unto man."*

It is written "Ask, and it shall be given you; seek, and ye shall find; knock, and it shall be opened unto you:" Mathew 7:7

Every time we *genuinely ask God in prayers* we get the right answer. The bible says *"For every one that asketh receiveth; and he that seeketh findeth; and to him that knocketh it shall be opened."* Mathew 7:8

Prayer is our only communication channel into the revelation of the things God has prepared for us in life. If you must hear from God, then you must be spiritual enough to pray without ceasing. When Peter was kept in prison, it was the church prayer that secured his release.

"Peter therefore was kept in prison: but prayer was made without ceasing of the church unto God for him." Acts12:5

"Until now you have not asked for anything in my name. Ask and you will receive, and your joy will be complete." John16:24

"If my people, which are called by my name, shall humble themselves, and pray, and seek my face, and turn from their wicked ways; then will I hear from heaven, and will forgive their sin, and will heal their land." 2chronicle7:14

Listen to me! A lot of people end up marrying the enemy because they never

Chapter 1: Asking God in Prayers for our God Ordained Spouse

prayed to God, about their spouse. For unless we ask God for the spouse ordained for us, we may end up marrying the wrong person. *Any marriage designed to last must be a marriage ordained by God. The word says… "I know that, whatsoever God doeth, it shall be forever:…"*

For unless we apply *divine wisdom* of God, any marriage that is not ordained by God is subject to fail. The scripture says, that *God is the author and finisher of our faith.* But God is also the author and finisher of marriage in my own opinion.

If you believe you are ready to marry, your first step must be to pray about it. It is a good idea, to have anyone who can pray for us, pray for us about our God ordained spouse. *"For unless you travail in prayers, you will not prevail with answers."*

WHAT ARE THE SECRETS OF LASTING MARRIAGE?

Interestingly a lot of couples have been together through thick, thin for decades, while other couples flounder right from the beginning.

1. *The Power of Intimacy*

To me, *Intimacy has Power*. Intimacy does not only mean sexual contacts or exercise. It includes emotional togetherness and wellness of the mind, spirit, soul, and body. *"But he that is joined unto the Lord is one spirit."* 1cor6:17

Intimacy between spouses, brings a mental and physical closeness that breaks down any unforeseen barriers like resentment, pride, envy, blame regret, rejection. Whenever spouses engage in altercation or succumb to arguments, Intimacy has great power to unite each other instantaneously. By this I mean, when both spouse are responsible in fulfilling other obligations in their career, academics, or, intimacy is easily be lost when couples work long hours.

For any spouse to preserve their marriage intimacy must become an ultimate goal. All couples must always come together to celebrate their love for each other on a daily bases.

Passion Fans the Flames

Spouses in long-lasting marriages *tend to share a passion for life,* as well as for each other. Passion heats things up in a good way. Certain neurotransmitters in the brain spike whether you're getting fervent over your favorite sports team or your spouse. When both spouse have passion for one time, they tend to come together always.

Wisdom for Marriage Stability

Forgive Each Other daily

We were told….

"For if ye forgive men their trespasses, your heavenly Father will also forgive you: But if ye forgive not men their trespasses, neither will your Father forgive your trespasses." **Mathew6:14-15**

Forgiving each other means more than taking a deep breath in the face of minor transgressions. To me, Forgiveness also means that you don't hang onto past baggage and past pain. Be willing to let go and to move forward with your lives. Accept your differences and don't try to change your spouse.

Spouse must be united

"Behold, how good and how pleasant it is for brethren to dwell together in unity! It is like the precious ointment upon the head, that ran down upon the beard, even Aaron's

beard: that went down to the skirts of his garments; As the dew of Hermon, and as the dew that descended upon the mountains of Zion: for there the Lord commanded the blessing, even life for evermore."
Psalms 133:1-3

From the above scripture every united family is a blessed family. Spouse must be united in times of crisis, joy, pain, and sorrow. Every time each spouse solely depend on another spouse for all financial and emotional support, it frustrate and puts more stress on that spouse

Spouses must be committed to God and each other

Commitment to God and to our marriage stabilizes our relationship. We must be committed to God and to our spouses. "Commit thy way unto the Lord; trust also in him; and he shall bring it to pass."
Psalms 37:5.

Wisdom for Marriage Stability

Be Friends

If your spouse is not your friend, then you have married your enemy. Our spouse must be our friend. Otherwise, how can you have fellowship, and relationship with a stranger? Our wife/husband must become our friend for an exciting and lasting relationship.

Do not be in a rush to marry

Again this is my personal opinion, do not be in a rush to get married to anyone regardless of their persuasion or influence. Marriage must be done by a free will and under the right conditions. Every time you rush into any relation. Remember "…he that believeth shall not make haste." **Isaiah28:16**

"Nevertheless, to avoid fornication, let every man have his own wife, and let every woman have her own husband.

Chapter1:AskingGodinPrayersforourGodOrdainedSpouse

Let the husband render unto the wife due benevolence: and likewise also the wife unto the husband.

The wife hath not power of her own body, but the husband: and likewise also the husband hath not power of his own body, but the wife.

> Defraud ye not one the other, except it be with consent for a time, that ye may give yourselves to fasting and prayer; and come together again, that Satan tempt you not for your incontinency."

1Cor7:2-5

Although the Love of God and *an-unconditional love for one another* .Every one of us must be able to forgive and forget in life. No matter what went wrong, learnt to say "I forgive you", and "I am sorry".

CHAPTER 2
UNDERSTANDING GOD'S CHOSEN SPOUSE FOR YOU

"The man that wandereth out of the way of understanding shall remain in the congregation of the dead." **Proverb 21:16**

"Good understanding giveth favour: but the way of transgressors is hard." **Proverb 13:15**

One of the greatest mystery whenever a man finds a wife, is the ability to understand *her personality completely*. God loves marriage. It has always been His design from the very beginning.

Marriage was not simply created for the purposes of pro-creation. God hates divorce and it is His intention that you marry the right person so that you may have a fruitful

Chapter 2: Understanding God's Chosen Spouse for You

partnership in His Kingdom. If you are already married.

If your spouse is not a Christian, pray into these areas and trust God to save them and work in the areas mentioned below.

Marriage is sowing ground where you sow your patience, love, enthusiasm and watch it multiply in those around you who celebrate your presence. Eyes require a view. Ears require sound. The mind requires thoughts. Aloneness creates vulnerability God knew it. "And the Lord said, it is not good that the man should be alone" **Gen 2:18.**

Consider the following in a relationship.

GOD IS A JEALOUS GOD AND DOES NOT SHARE HIS GLORY

Your Spouse is not responsible for your joy. The presence of God creates your joy. "In Thy presence is fullness of joy"" Psalm

16:11. Your spouse is a gift from God to you. Honor Him or her. But they must not be worshipped or take the place of God in your life. They are God's gift into your life. That gift is intended to protect your focus, reduce distractions, and create a climate of protection.

Focus often creates blindness. When you are looking North, you cannot see South. Someone else is needed for your protection, so, God provides the gift of a mate. Unfortunately, some who qualify for our attention are often unqualified to receive our heart.

If You Do Not Possess A Passionate Desire To Give To Them. The proof of love is the desire to give. Jesus explained it. "For God so loved the world, that He gave His only begotten Son…" John 3:16. Too often, marriage becomes an exchange. Exchange is the evidence of business, not love. You should desire to give time, God's gift to you.

Chapter 2: Understanding God's Chosen Spouse for You

If They Do Not Possess A Passionate Desire To Give Back To You. I am not referring to expensive gifts, money or clothes. A listening ear, flexibility, patience and the willingness to be corrected are gifts.

If Your Personal Achievements Do Not Create Excitement In Them. When good things happen, who is the first person you desire to phone? Pay attention to that. Celebration is a compass. Those you love to celebrate with are clues to the puzzle of your life. When uncommon love exists, uncommon celebration is normal. Uncommon love does not compete with the success of another. It tastes and savours and enjoys the pleasure of another.

If They Never Ask Quality Questions Concerning Your Greatest Dreams And Goals.

Questions reveal desire. Questions reveal humility.

If They Ignore Worthy Counsel From Qualified Mentors In Their Life. Who are their heroes? You become like those you admire. You adapt the habits of those you envy. Who is their dominant mentor? At whose feet do they sit consistently? If they rebel against the counsel of their pastor, they are living undisciplined, uncovered, and unadvised. Tragedy is scheduled.

If You Do Not See Continuous Improvement In The Relationship. Improvement is revealed by the decrease of conflict. Conflict occurs through opposite goals, philosophies, or beliefs. Bonding should increase unity and brings a decrease in contention and strife. Strife is the evidence of opposite belief systems.

If They Show Little Remorse Concerning Their Past Mistakes And Sins. Repentant people are not arrogant. Repentant people do not blame others for their decisions. Memories of mistakes

Chapter 2: Understanding God's Chosen Spouse for You

should produce sorrow and heartache. When regret is not expressed the offence usually occurs again. Some people never repent for the past mistakes. Why? They have not tasted the painful consequences of their rebellion. They do not possess a true fear of God. They believe they are beyond judgement. It is futile to pursue a relationship with someone who does not possess an obvious fear of God. Uncorrected conduct becomes repeated conduct.

The fear of God keeps a mate faithful. Beauty will not. Your beauty does not make another woman ugly. Beauty cannot guarantee faithfulness, the fear of God keeps us faithful. It saddens me to watch some mentors of women teach the art of manipulation, intimidation and deception to deceive the men they are pursuing. You'll never respect anyone you are capable of deceiving.

If They Have An Obsession To Attract The Attention Of The Opposite Sex. Some women are unhappy unless every man in the room gravitates around her as the 'centre of attention.' I have known men who cannot pass by a mirror without being mesmerised by their perceived beauty.

If Breaking The Law Is Exciting To Them. When I see a radar detector on the dash of a car, I recognise that I am in the presence of someone who despises restraint, sneers at the law and wants the world to know it.

When It Is Obvious That You Will Never Become Their Focus And Assignment. They may enjoy you, laugh with you and like you. They may even be trustworthy as a confidante. But, a spouse is a different matter. When God brings you a spouse, that person becomes your Assignment. The wife of a young preacher was agitated and frustrated. As we drove

Chapter 2: Understanding God's Chosen Spouse for You

home from a crusade late one night, she looked at me with great exasperation and said, "I must find out what my Assignment is!" I replied gently, "He is there beside you. God calls him your husband. He is your Assignment. You are his Assignment." Many marriages of ministers are fragmented today. Good men and women of God are often in miserable marriages. Publicly, their life looks glamorous, but they despise their marriage because they have ceased to view the other as their true Assignment.

THEY MUST TRUST IN GOD AND TRUST YOU ALSO.

Whoever you admire, you submit to. Loyalty comes with humility in life. Every time you notice insubordination in the marriage hierarchy. *Take heed lest you fall into temptation.*

If They Have Not Exited Previous Relationships Peaceably. Many thrive on strife. They will destroy anything they cannot own or control. Peace bores them. Silence nauseates them. Warfare is their fuel. They will speak any words necessary to find the boundary lines around them. It'll be impossible to have an enjoyable marriage.

If Their Parents Have Contempt For You Or Your Assignment In Life. The bloodline is more powerful than anyone can imagine. It is spiritual thing. It is a spirit connection. God arranged it Himself. So, you may marry a rebel who even despises his parents, but when crisis comes, he will reach back to the bloodline for affirmation. If you marry someone whose parents look condescendingly upon you because of your lack of education, social class or finances, remember that they will be the third party always speaking into the heart of your spouse.

If They Refuse To Sit Consistently Under The Mentorship Of A Spiritual

Chapter 2: Understanding God's Chosen Spouse for You

Leader. Changes will not occur without mentors or uncommon pains. Unwillingness to sit under the mentorship of a man of God is a devastating revelation of potential failure.

If Their Own Dreams Are Not Big Enough To Motivate Them. If they can sleep all day, watch television all night and refuse to produce anything significant with their life - you better think twice before pouring your life into them. Every person should have a dream big enough to get him out of bed in the morning.

If They Are Uncomfortable In The Presence Of God. You can date a man who is handsome and brings you flowers– but if he hates the presence of God, there is no hope of greatness ever being birthed within him. The man you see will never be more than what he is today. Preachers will become his rivals. He will become intimidated by your church attendance. Unsaved men are often intimidated by believing men because they know in their heart that a man who walks with God has something they lack.

If They Feel Inferior To You. True, everyone is superior to others in some way. But, it is important that those who walk beside you feel confident, qualified, and called of God to be your mate.

If They Do Not Long To Understand And Pleasure You. Uncommon love longs to pleasure another. Uncommon love seeks every opportunity to communicate itself. What do you enjoy? Where do you want to go for vacation? What's your favorite flower? Your spouse should long to know.

If Continuous Strife Exists Between Them And Their Parents. Honoring our parents was the first commandment with a promise. Those who celebrate the authority over their life ultimately succeed.

Introduction

If They Treat The Favour Of Others With Ingratitude. Countless times, I have paid for meals at restaurants and never received a single thanks for it. I dated a lady for many months without receiving a thank you for anything I purchased or did for her during that year. Her explanation, "I simply wasn't taught to say the word 'Thanks.' I will show it in other ways." Absurd.

If They Do Not Hunger To Know The Voice Of God. Obedience is the secret of every successful person. If a man or a woman disdains The Voice of Truth and Wisdom (The Bible) – they will birth a parade of tragedies and catastrophes. Their decisions will create losses. Their weakness will flourish. Unlawful desire will rage like an inferno. Such a marriage is a path to spiritual suicide.

If You Are Not Excited About Introducing Them To Those You Love. When you are truly in love, that's all you want to talk about. Are you ashamed? Be truthful with yourself...

If They Show Little Respect For The Battles You Have Won Throughout Your Lifetime. Have you mastered prejudice, fear or poverty? When someone loves you, they admire your achievements.

If Conversation With Them Has Become Burdensome. I have been with some who left me frazzled, exhausted and I did not know why. Right people energise you. Wrong people exhaust you. True love will motivate you.

If Your Time Spent With Them Always Ends With Guilt Or Disappointment. Withdrawal from any relationship occurs if guilt, fear or a sense of entrapment emerges.

If People Of Excellence Do Not Surround Them. Study the kinds of people that your potential mate finds enjoyable.

Chapter 2: Understanding God's Chosen Spouse for You

That is a clue to their life and your future with them.

If They Are Unwilling To Follow Your Personal Advice And Counsel. A Godly wife is The Prophetess in the bosom of her husband. A husband should be a Well of Wisdom for his wife.

If You Do Not Admire And Respect The Mentor At Whose Feet They Sit. Their mentor is feeding either strength or a weakness. If you opposed their mentor, a happy marriage is impossible.

If They Continuously Give You Counsel Contrary To The Word Of God. The Word of God is Truth. It withstands any test. It destroys wrong desire within you. It unleashes your faith. It produces hope. It purifies your mind. It is the master key to all success on earth. Your reaction to God's Word determines God's reaction to His own children. (Hosea 4:6) God will become their enemy if they continue to defy His Word. It would be tragic to bond with someone God has no fellowship with.

If Their Presence Does Not Motivate You To A Higher Level Of Excellence. You already possess weaknesses. You do not require anyone to feed them. Anyone can pull you down. That is why God gives you a spouse to lift you up.

If You Cannot Trust Them With The Knowledge Of Your Greatest Weakness. Each of us contains weaknesses that embarrass us. We despise them. It may be anger, fear, or lust. Your mate is there to strengthen you, not weaken you. If you believe it is necessary to hide your weakness instead of share it, you may have the wrong mate.

If You Cannot Trust Them With Your Finances. This narrows down the field considerably, doesn't it! Do not bond your

Chapter 2: Understanding God's Chosen Spouse for You

life with someone too immature to handle the importance of financial responsibility. One young man explained to me, "I do not want my fiancée to know anything about my money or she will spend it. As soon as she discovers I have extra money, she persuades me to run up my credit cards."

If You Cannot Trust Them With Your Most Painful Memories. Every person is running from a painful memory. Millionaires often share that their days of poverty have motivated them. Their painful memories have driven them to uncommon achievement. Some explain a father who beat them mercilessly. It left them marked forever. Memories are keys to understanding each other.

If You Cannot Trust Them With Your Greatest Fears Or Secrets. Fear often limits us. It should motivate us to change. It may be the fear of flying, or the dark. It may be a fear of dying with disease. Whatever it is – think twice if their love is not strong enough to destroy fear. "Perfect love casteth out fear:" 1 John 4:18.

If You Cannot Trust Them Around Your Friends. Flirtation is deadly. The death of many marriages begins with flirtation. It is not harmless. Ever.

If You Cannot Trust Them In Your Absence. Jealousy is a cruel dictator and tyrant. It is often unfounded and produced by a painful memory of disloyalty or betrayal. I have seen many marriages unravel because of a deep sense of distrust. Note the signals.

Choose your spouse wisely

If you have identified with the gift and calling of God upon your life, then you must know who is qualified to be your God ordained spouse. Recognition of our God chosen spouse is a great blessing to our career and destiny.

Chapter 2: Understanding God's Chosen Spouse for You

We were told…..

Whoso findeth a wife findeth a good thing, and obtaineth favour of the Lord.

We were also told …….

"I will praise thee; for I am fearfully and wonderfully made: aviorus are thy works; and that my soul knoweth right well." Pslams139:14

"Submitting yourselves one to another in the fear of God." Ephesians5:21

"Wives, submit yourselves unto your own husbands, as unto the Lord." Ephesians5:22

" For the husband is the head of the wife, even as Christ is the head of the church: and he is the avior of the body." Ephesians5:23

"Therefore as the church is subject unto Christ, so let the wives be to their own husbands in everything." Ephesians5:24

"Husbands, love your wives, even as Christ also loved the church, and gave himself for it;" Ephesians5:25

"Wherefore they are no more twain, but one flesh. What therefore God hath joined together, let not man put asunder." Mathew19:6

CONCLUSION

"Wherefore they are no more twain, but one flesh. What therefore God hath joined together, let not man put asunder. **Mathew19:6**

"Two are better than one; because they have a good reward for their labour."

"For if they fall, the one will lift up his fellow: but woe to him that is alone when he falleth; for he hath not another to help him up."

Chapter 2: Understanding God's Chosen Spouse for You

"Again, if two lie together, then they have heat: but how can one be warm alone?"

"And if one prevail against him, two shall withstand him; and a threefold cord is not quickly broken. " **Ecll4:9-12**

"Therefore if any man be in Christ, he is a new creature: old things are passed away; behold, all things are become new".

2cor5:17

Now repeat this Prayer after me

Say Lord Jesus, I accept you today, as my Lord and my savior, forgive me of my sins wash me with your blood. Right now, I believe, I am sanctified, I am save, I am free, I am free from the Power of sin to serve the Lord Jesus. Thank you Lord for saving me. Amen.

Wisdom for Marriage Stability

What must I do to determine my divine visitation?

To determine divine visitation you must be born again! The word says as many as received him, to them gave He power to become the sons of God. Even to them that believe on his name.

To qualify for divine visitation do the following sincerely

1) Acknowledge that you are a sinner and that He died for you. Rom 3:23.

2) Repent of your sins. Acts 3:19, Luke13:5, 2Peter3:9

3) Believe in your heart that Jesus died for your sin. Romans 10:10

4) Confess Jesus as the Lord over your life. Romans10:10, Acts2:21

I will strongly recommend that you become an active member of this prayer ministry.

Chapter 2: Understanding God's Chosen Spouse for You

WISDOM KEYS

Every Productive Society is a society heading to the top

Millions of Nigerians run away from Nigeria, very few Nigerians stay in Nigeria.

My decision to return Nigeria is the will of God for my life

My short coming in America after 18 years, trained me to be wise, to think, reflect and reason appropriately.

If you train your mind to reason it will train your hands to earn money.

It is absurd to use the money of the heathen to build the kingdom of the living God.

Every Ministry reveals its agenda and goal either at the beginning or at the end. Be careful of your life it is your first Ministry.

The average American mind is conditioned for a continual quest to get new things and (discard the former) and throw away old things.

When I considered well, my BMW jeep became my initial deposit for the work of the ministry in Nigeria

Everyone is waiting for you to change your mind until you change your thinking nothing changes around you.

Multiple academic degrees in other discipline gave me the chance to think, reflect, and reason

What so everyone are thinking and reflecting at the moment reveals you to the time and the now factor

All events and intents are the product of precise thought processes, accurate reason every event is designed for a designated timeline

Chapter 2: Understanding God's Chosen Spouse for You

Wisdom is your ability to think, to create and invent. If you can think wise enough you will come out of penury

The distance between you and success is your creative ability to think reason and reflect accurate.

Success is the result of hard work, commitment resolve, and determination learning from past mistakes and failing.

If you organize your mind you have organized your life and destiny.

There is a thin line between success and failure. If you look above and beyond you are on your way to success.

Wealth is your ability to think, power is your ability to reason and success is your ability to be informed.

If you can make use of your mind by thinking and reasoning God will make use of your life and destiny.

Think and Be Great

Reflect, Reason, think and be great

Famous people are born of woman

That you will make it is your intention; that you will survive is your resolve, that you will succeed with changes is your determination, personal efforts and hard work.

No man was born a failure. Lack of vision is the end product of failure.

Working with mental patients encourages and aspire me to be a productive observant and dedicated to my assignment.

Successful people are not magicians, it is the will power combined with hard work, and determination and a resolve to succeed that make them succeed.

In the unequivocal state of the mind, intention is not a location or a position it is the state of the mind.

Chapter 2: Understanding God's Chosen Spouse for You

So many people think that they think. The mind is used to think reflect and reason. You will remain blind with your eye open until you can see with your mind by thinking.

There is no favoritism in accurate and precise calculation

Although knowledge is power, information is the key and gateway to a great future.

It will take the hand of God to move the hand of man.

With the backing of the great wise God, nothing will disconnect you from your inheritance.

As long as you have wisdom and understanding of God, Satan and evil cannot manipulate your life and destiny.

You have come this far by yourself judgment and decision you have made in the past, now lean and listen to God for another dimension of greatness.

Great people are common people it is extra ordinary effort and the price of sacrifice that produces greatness.

As a mental direct care worker I saw a great pastor and a motivational speaker within myself.

Menial job does not reduce your self-worth, until you resolve to achieve greatness see greatness in all you do; you will never count in your community.

The principle of Jesus will solve your gambling and addiction problems

The man of Jesus will lead you into heaven,

Everyone have their self-appraisal and what they think about you. Until you discover yourself other opinion about you will alter the real you.

Chapter 2: Understanding God's Chosen Spouse for You

Supervisors and directors are just a position in the chain of command in a work place. Never allow your supervisor hierarchy to alter your opinion about yourself.

Everyone can come out of debt if they make up their mind.

That I am not a decision maker at work does not diminish my contribution to my world.

Although it appears like it was a poor decision to accept a direct care employment at a psychiatric hospital as I reflect of my nine years of experience, it became apparent that I have learnt and experienced enough for my next assignment.

Self-encouragement and determination is a resolve of the heart.

If you are determined to make a difference, and do the things that make a difference you will eventually make a difference.

Good things do not come easy

Short cuts will cut your life short.

Those who look ahead move ahead.

Life is all about making an impact. In your life time strive to make an impact in your community.

Make friends and connect with people who are moving ahead of you in life.

If you can look around well you have come a long way in your life, made a lot of difference and realized a lot of success in life.

If you are my old friend, hurry up to reach out to me before I become a stranger to you.

Everything I am blessed with inspirations from God, that change my

Chapter 2: Understanding God's Chosen Spouse for You

definition and interpretation of the world around me.

I thought I was stagnant and lonely until I looked around and noticed my children running around and my wife cooking.

At 40 I resigned my Job to seek the Lord forever.

My ministry took a drastic rise to the top when the wisdom of God visited me with knowledge and understanding.

You will be a better person if you understand the characteristics of your personality – your mood swings attitudes and habits.

It is the seed of love you sow into the heart of a child and a woman that you reap in due time.

Love is not selfish, love share everything including the concealed secrets of the mind.

As long as you have a prayer life and a bible; you will never feel lonely, rejected, and idle in the race of life.

When good friends disconnect from you, let them go, they might have seen something new in a different direction.

Confidence in yourself and in God is the only way to bring you out of captivity

Never train a child to waste his/her time.

The mind is the greatest assets of a great future.

You walk by common sense run by principles and fly by instruction.

Those who fly in flight of life fly alone.

I have seen a tolling vehicle I have seen a tolling ship I have never seen a tolling airplane.

I exercise my judgment and make a decision every minute of the day.

Chapter 2: Understanding God's Chosen Spouse for You

Decisions are crucial, critica,l and vital with reference to your future.

So many people wish for a great future. You can only work towards a great future.

Your celebrity status began when you discovered your talent. What are you good at? Work at it with all commitment.

Prayers will sustain you but the wisdom of God will prosper you.

When I met Oyedepo, his teachings changed my perspective, but when I met Ibiyeomie; His teaching changed my perception.

I will be successful in ministry if only I concentrate and focus my energy in the work of the ministry.

It took the late Dr. Vincent Pearle Norman's book to open my mind towards kingdom success.

CHAPTER 3
PRAYER OF SALVATION

"Neither is there salvation in any other: for there is none other name under heaven given among men, whereby we must be saved."

Acts 4:12

The purpose of this book is for us to receive genuine salvation. If you have read all through this book without a decision for Jesus Christ, then the purpose has been defeated.

Salvation means deliverance from sin and evil forces of destruction. It is my prayer that you embrace the Lord today. We are excited as a prayer family to hear of your testimony.

Chapter 3 : Prayer of Salvation

"Now when they heard this, they were pricked in their heart, and said unto Peter and to the rest of the apostles, Men and brethren, what shall we do? Then Peter said unto them, Repent, and be baptized every one of you in the name of Jesus Christ for the remission of sins, and ye shall receive the gift of the Holy Ghost." Acts2:37-38

"And they said, Believe on the Lord Jesus Christ, and thou shalt be saved, and thy house." Acts16:30.

It is my prayer for you to make a decision today for Jesus Christ. Join a bible believing church or you can join us. We prayer online every Monday and Wednesday 9:00pm to 10:00pm 515-739-1216 code 162288.

You can worship with us 343sanford Avenue. Wednesdays-Bible study-7pm-9pm, Fridays 10:45pm-1am Encounter night, Sundays 10:45am-12:45pm anointing service.

MIRACLE CARE OUTREACH

> "...But that the members should have the same care one for another"
>
> **1cor12:25**

We are all members of the body of Christ. Jesus commanded us to love our neighbor as ourselves. This includes caring for one another as a member of one body. True love is expressed in caring and giving. The word says for God so Love He gave….

Reach out to someone in need of Jesus, help someone in crisis find Christ. Look out and prove your love to Jesus by caring and inviting your friends and associates to find Jesus the Healer.

Chapter 3 : Prayer of Salvation

Invite your friends to our Home Care Cell Fellowship (Miracle chapel Intl Satellite fellowship) In the USA at 343 Sanford Avenue Newark New Jersey 07106.

If you are in Nigeria—**MIRACLE OF GOD MINISTRIES**

A.K.A "**MIRACLE CHAPEL INTL**" Mpama –Egbu-Owerri Imo state Nigeria.

(Home Care Cell fellowship Group). We meet every Tuesday at 6:00pm-7:00pm.

LIFE IS NOT ALL ABOUT DURATION BUT ITS ALL ABOUT DONATION

What does the above statement mean?....

Life consists not in accumulation of material wealth..Luke12:15. But it's all about liberality….meaning- what you can give and share with others. Proverb11:25. When you live for others–You live forever-because you out live your generation by the legacy you live behind after you depart into glory to be with the Lord. But when you live to yourself – you are reduced to self—you are easily forgotten when you die and depart in glory. Permit me to admonish you today to live your life to be a blessing to a soul connected to you today. I want you to know that so many souls are connected and looking up to you, and through you so many souls will be saved and rescued from destruction. Will you disciple someone today to find Jesus Christ?

As a genuine Christian; it is your duty to evangelize Jesus Christ to all you meet on your way. Jesus is still in the healing business-Jesus is still doing miracles from time of old to now. Therefore tell someone about Jesus Christ today, disciple and bring them to Church. John 1:45 Philip findeth Nathanael….

Chapter 3 : Prayer of Salvation

Please to prove the sincerity of your love for God today; please become a soul winner. The dignity of your Christianity is hidden in your boldness to proclaim and evangelize Jesus Christ to all you meet on your way. There is a question mark on the integrity of your Christianity until you become a life soul winner. Invite someone to join us worship the Lord Jesus this coming Sunday. Amen

MIRACLE OF GOD MINISTRIES
PILLARS OF THE COMMISSION

We Believe Preach and Practice the following

1) We believe and preach Salvation to every living human being

2) We believe and preach Repentance and forgiveness of sins

3) We believe and preach the baptism of the Holy Spirit and Spiritual gifts

4) We believe and teach the Prosperity

5) We believe and preach Divine Healing and Miracles (Signs &Wonder)

6) We believe and preach Faith

7) We believe and Proclaim the Power of God (Supernatural)

8) We believe and Proclaim Praise& Worship to God

9) We believe and preach Wisdom

10) We believe and preach Holiness (Consecration)

11) We believe and preach Vision

12) We believe and teach the Word of God

13) We believe and teach Success

14) We believe and practice Prayer

15) We believe and teach Deliverance

Chapter 3 : Prayer of Salvation

This 15 stones form the Pillars of Our Commission. Become part of this church family and follow this great move of God.

MY HEART FELT PRAYER FOR YOU

I believe you have a new testimony already. I pray God seal your testimony in Jesus Name. Amen

Now let me Pray for you:

Sweet Holy Spirit, I give you thanks and praise for my spouse. Lord strengthen and empower us together to love you and ourselves more and more forever more.

Lord Jesus I thank you for life. Father grant us the serenity, and wisdom to know the right thing to do, concerning our spouse at any prevailing difficult times. I thank you for you have heard me. In Jesus mighty name. Amen

CHAPTER 4

ABOUT THE AUTHOR

Rev Franklin N Abazie is the founding and Presiding Pastor of Miracle of God Ministries with headquarters in Newark, New Jersey USA and a branch church in Owerri-Imo State Nigeria. He is following the footsteps of one of his mentors, Oral Roberts (Healing Evangelist) of the blessed memory. The Lord passed Oral Roberts healing mantle two days before he went to be with the Lord at age 91 into the hand of healing evangelist-Rev Franklin N Abazie in a vision.

In all his services the Power and Presence of God is present to heal all in his audience. He is an ordained man of God with a Healing Ministry reviving the healing and miracle ministry of Jesus Christ of Nazareth.

Pastor Franklin N Abazie, is called by God with a unique mandate: **"THE**

Chapter 4 : Prayer of Salvation

MOMENT IS DUE TO IMPACT YOUR WORLD THROUGH THE REVIVAL OF THE HEALING & MIRACLE MINISTRY OF JESUS CHRIST OF NAZARETH

I AM SENDING YOU TO RESTORE HEALTH UNTO THEE AND I WILL HEAL THEE OF THY WOUNDS. SAID THE LORD OF HOST"

He is a gifted ardent Teacher of the word of God who operates also in the office of a Prophet, generating and attracting undeniable signs & wonders, special miracles and healings, with apostolic fireworks of the Holy Ghost. He is the founding and presiding senior Pastor of this fast growing Healing ministry. He has written over 86 inspirational, healing and transforming books covering almost all aspect of divine healing and life. He is happily married and blessed with children.

BOOKS BY REV FRANKLIN N ABAZIE

1) Commanding Abundance
2) The outcome of faith
3) Understanding the secret of prevailing prayers.
4) Understanding the secret of the man God uses
5) Activating my due Season
6) Overcoming Divine Verdicts
7) The Outcome of Divine Wisdom
8) Understanding God's Restoration Mandate
9) Walking in the Victory and Authority of the truth
10) Gods Covenant Exemption
11) Destiny Restoration Pillars

Books By Rev Franklin N Abazie

12) Provoking Acceptable Praise
13) Understanding Divine Judgment
14) Activating Angelic Re-enforcement
15) Provoking Un-Merited Favor
16) The Benefits of the Speaking faith
17) Understanding Divine Arrangement
18) Understanding Divine Healing
19) The Mystery of Endurance
20) Obeying Divine Instructions
21) Understanding the Voice of God
22) Never give up on Hope
23) The prevailing Power of faith
24) Understanding Divine Prosperity
25) The Reward of Prayer
26) Covenant Keys to Answered Prayers
27) Activating the Forces of Vengeance

28) Put your faith to work
29) Where is your trust?
30) The Audacity of the Blood of Jesus
31) Redeeming Your Days
32) The Force of Vision
33) Breaking the shackles of Family curses
34) Wisdom for Marriage Stability
35) Overcoming Prevailing challenges
36) The Prayer solution
37) The Power of Prayer
38) The effective strategy of Prayer
41) The Prayer that works
42) Walking in Forgiveness
43) The Power of Persistence
44) Overcoming Divine verdicts
45) The audacity of the blood of Jesus.

Books By Rev Franklin N Abazie

46) The prevailing power of the blood of Jesus
47) The benefit of the speaking faith.
48) Fearless faith
49) Redeeming Your Days.
50) The Supernatural Power of Prophecy
51) The companionship of the Holy Spirit
52) Understanding Divine Judgement
53) Understanding Divine Prosperity
54) Dominating Controlling Forces
54) The winner's Faith
55) Destiny Restoration Pillars
56) Developing Spiritual Muscles
57) Inexplicable faith
58) The lifestyle of Prayer
59) Developing a positive attitude in life.

60) The mystery of Divine supply
61) Encounter with the Power of God
62) Walking in love
63) Praying in the Spirit
64) How to provoke your testimony
65) Walking in the reality of the anointing
66) The Reality of new birth
67) The Price of freedom
68) The Supernatural power of faith
69) The intellectual components of Redemption.
70) Overcoming Fear
71) Overcoming Prevailing Challenges
72) My life & Ministry
73) The Mystery of Praise
74) The Power of Decision

Books By Rev Franklin N Abazie

75) Overcoming the memories of Divorce

76) The lifestyle of Praise

77) The Law of focus

78) Dream Big

79) The Power of Dedication

79) The Power of Discipline

80) Pressing towards Perfection

81) The Prevailing Power of Hope

82) The Power of Determination

MIRACLE OF GOD MINISTRIES

NIGERIA CRUSADE
2012

MIRACLE OF GOD MINISTRIES

NIGERIA CRUSADE
2012

MIRACLE OF GOD MINISTRIES

*NIGERIA CRUSADE
2012*

www.ingramcontent.com/pod-product-compliance
Lightning Source LLC
Chambersburg PA
CBHW021135300426
44113CB00006B/438